Wheels at Work

Focus: Designing, Making and Appraising
Materials
Systems

PETER SLOAN &
SHERYL SLOAN

Fill a big box with books. Now try to push it along the ground. The box is heavy and hard to move.

Empty the box. Then put it on a skateboard. Fill the box with books.
It is easy to roll the box along on the wheels.

3

Big, heavy trains have steel wheels. These wheels roll along easily on the smooth rails.

An airplane has very strong wheels. It uses its wheels for taking off and landing. The wheels help the plane roll smoothly along the ground.

Bicycles have two light wheels. A bicycle can roll easily on a flat road. Some bicycle wheels are made for rough ground.

6

A dump truck is very
heavy. It has lots of big
wheels. The wheels are
made to roll over rough
ground.

7

People do not have wheels. People have feet. But people use skates, skateboards, and in-line skates to make them go fast!

8